"ALWAYS CREATE YOUR OWN DREAMS AND LIVE YOUR LIFE TO THE FULLEST."

—Susan Polis Schutz

❦

DREAM YOUR DREAMS . . . MAKE THEM HAPPEN. BELIEVE . . . AND BEGIN!

❦

"In high emotion . . . the reigning star is Susan Polis Schutz."
—Time

❦

"Susan Polis Schutz remains one of the most popular poets in America today, and her work touches virtually everyone."
—Associated Press

❦

"Susan's work continues to touch the hearts of millions across the world, sharing patience and joy, peace and love with people everywhere. . . . In a world filled with uncertainty, war and disease, famine and fear, Susan Polis Schutz is reminding people that a little love can go a long way."
—True Story

❦

"Susan Polis Schutz's popularity can be attributed to her ability to verbalize intimate, honest emotions shared but unsaid by most people. Her ability to write simply and honestly of the deepest emotions and the most fragile and fleeting moments strikes a responsive chord with readers."
—Woman's Day

❦

"A poet of the heart."
—Family Weekly

Books by Susan Polis Shutz

To My Son With Love

To My Daughter With Love

I Love You

Also edited by Susan Polis Shutz

Mother, I Will Always Love You

Published by
WARNER BOOKS

Don't Ever Stop Dreaming Your Dreams

A New Collection of Poems

Edited by Susan Polis Schutz

WARNER BOOKS

A Time Warner Company

Warner Books, Inc., 666 Fifth Avenue, New York, NY 10103

A Time Warner Company

Printed in the United States of America

First printing: October 1991

10 9 8 7 6 5 4 3 2 1

LIBRARY OF CONGRESS CATALOGING-IN-PUBLICATION DATA
Don't ever stop dreaming your dreams : a new collection of poems / edited by Susan Polis Schutz.
    p.   cm.
    ISBN 0-446-39319-3
    1. Friendship--Poetry.   2. Love poetry.   I. Schutz, Susan Polis.
    PN611.F8D6   1991
    811.008'0353--dc20   91-18763
                                          CIP

CONTENTS

Don't Ever Stop Dreaming
Your Dreams

*Don't ever try to understand everything—
some things will just never make sense.
Don't ever be reluctant to show your feelings—
when you're happy, give in to it!
When you're not, live with it.
Don't ever be afraid to try to make
    things better—
you might be surprised at the results.
Don't ever take the weight of the world
    on your shoulders.
Don't ever feel threatened by the future—
take life one day at a time.
Don't ever feel guilty about the past—
    what's done is done. Learn from any
    mistake you might have made.
Don't ever feel that you are alone—
    there is always somebody there for you
    to reach out to.
Don't ever forget that you can achieve
    so many of the things you can
    imagine— imagine that!
It's not as hard as it seems.
Don't ever stop loving,
    don't ever stop believing,
        don't ever stop dreaming your
        dreams.*

—Laine Parsons

Find Happiness
in Everything You Do

*P*eople will get only what they seek
Choose your goals carefully
Know what you like
and what you do not like
Be critical about what you can do well
and what you cannot do well
Choose a career or lifestyle that interests you
and work hard to make it a success
but also have fun in what you do
Be honest with people
    and help them if you can
but don't depend on anyone
    to make life easy or happy for you
(only you can do that for yourself)
Be strong and decisive
but remain sensitive
Regard your family and the idea of a family
as the basis for security, support and love

Understand who you are
and what you want in life
before sharing your life with someone
When you are ready to enter a relationship
make sure that the person is worthy of
everything you are physically and mentally

Strive to achieve all that you want
Find happiness in everything you do
Love with your entire being
Love with an uninhibited soul
Make a triumph
of every aspect
of your life

—Susan Polis Schutz

One Step at a Time
Is the Best Way to Go

*When going through life
and traveling in the direction
of your dreams, the best way
to get ahead is the simplest way:*

Take it one step at a time.

*Don't look over your shoulder; if you do,
you'll feel the weight of all your
yesterdays upon you.
And don't worry about what lies ahead.
By the time you get to
the bend in the road
or the crest of the hill,
you're going to be better and stronger
than you ever were before.*

*Just go a step at a time,
one day at a time.
And you'll find a rich, thankful life
you never thought you could afford.*

—Adrian Rogers

Keep Believing in Yourself
and Your Special Dreams

There may be days
when you get up in the morning
and things aren't the way
you had hoped they would be.
That's when you have to
tell yourself that things
will get better.
There are times when people
disappoint you and let you down,
but those are the times
when you must remind yourself
to trust your own judgments
and opinions,
to keep your life focused on
believing in yourself
and all that you are capable of.
There will be challenges to face
and changes to make in your life,
and it is up to you to accept them.
Constantly keep yourself headed
in the right direction for you.

It may not be easy at times,
but in those times of struggle
you will find a stronger sense
of who you are,
and you will also see yourself
developing into the person
you have always wanted to be.

Life is a journey through time,
filled with many choices;
each of us will experience life
in our own special way.
So when the days come
that are filled with frustration
and unexpected responsibilities,
remember to believe in yourself
and all you want your life to be,
because the challenges and changes
will only help you to find
the dreams that you know
are meant to come true for you.

—Deanna Beisser

You are your own greatest asset—
there is nothing you cannot do.
No one can keep you from dreaming
your dreams, and only you can
prevent them from coming true.
Your achievements are not
determined by your ability alone,
but by the desire you possess
to reach them. There are no worlds
outside of those you create for
yourself, and the only
boundaries are those you
establish and choose to live within.
Never be afraid to defend your
decisions, regardless. No one can
possibly know what is best for you
other than yourself.

—Terry Everton

Always Create Your Own Dreams and Live Your Life to the Fullest

Dreams can come true
if you take the time to
think about what you want in life
Get to know yourself
Find out who you are
Choose your goals carefully
Be honest with yourself
Always believe in yourself
Find many interests and pursue them
Find out what is important to you
Find out what you are good at
Don't be afraid to make mistakes
Work hard to achieve successes
When things are not going right
don't give up—just try harder
Find courage inside of you to remain strong
Give yourself freedom to try out new things
Don't be so set in your ways that you can't grow
Always act in an ethical way

Laugh and have a good time
Form relationships with people you respect
Treat others as you want them to treat you
Be honest with people
Accept the truth
Speak the truth
Open yourself up to love
Don't be afraid to love
Remain close to your family
Take part in the beauty of nature
Be appreciative of all that you have
Help those less fortunate than you
Try to make other lives happy
Work towards peace in the world
Live life to the fullest
Create your own dreams
and your dreams will become
a reality

—Susan Polis Schutz

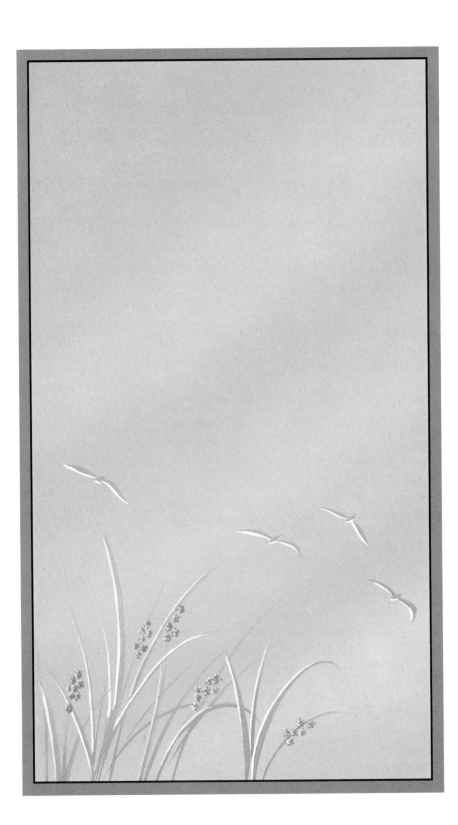

May Life's Greatest Gifts Always Be Yours...

Happiness. Deep down within.
Serenity. With each sunrise.
Success. In each facet of your life.
Close and caring friends.
Love. That never ends.

Special memories. Of all the yesterdays.
A bright today. With much to
   be thankful for.
A path. That leads to beautiful tomorrows.

And dreams. That do their best to come true.

—Collin McCarty

True Happiness in Life Comes When You Believe in Yourself

*O*ne of the most valuable lessons
you can ever learn in life is that
what you want
isn't always what you need.
You reach a point
    in your life when
you come to understand yourself
for the real feelings
you hold inside your heart,
not the feelings
that others want you to have.
When you begin to learn
what life means to you,
and how you are going to spend
your time and energy,
you realize that life is
only what you believe it to be.

If you want happiness,
then it is up to you
to make yourself happy
and not wait for someone else
to do it for you.
In the end, no one else
can make you happy;
happiness comes from within.
It is enjoying life for yourself
and appreciating others
as they join you in the things you do.
You may learn a lot
of different lessons in your life,
but the most important of all
is realizing that life is
everything you want it to be;
you just have to believe in yourself,
believe in others,
believe in your dreams,
and enjoy the changes of life
as they come your way.

—Nick Santana

In the pursuit of any dream,
there will be moments
when it seems that the dream is lost.
It is then that you must have faith
in the person that you are.
Believe that you have
the ability to overcome
any obstacle standing in your way,
and when your dream comes true,
you will realize then
what a stronger person
you have become.

—Lynn Brown

Always Be True to Yourself

*Take time to know yourself.
Make time to be with yourself,
   and learn to love yourself.
Remember it is not only important
   to give to others,
   but learn to give to yourself.
When you find yourself doubting,
   be confident.
When you feel like nothing
   is going right,
   do not despair.
Be patient with yourself—
   all in good time, situations
   will become clearer.*

Be true to yourself,
  and don't ever give up.
Continue to dream your dreams,
  because you are the one who can
  make them come true.
Be prepared to fall,
  but always get back up
  and try again.
Be prepared to succeed.
Trust yourself,
  and believe that you are
  capable and deserve the best.
Always listen to your heart.
Don't ever forget—
  you are a very special person.

—Randey Fisher

You Have Within You
the Courage
to Achieve Your Goals

You should always be assured
that your life
is of great worth.
There are those
who would have you give up,
but remember that dreams are cut short
only by those with no vision.
Your challenges are not over yet.
You must still prepare and grow.
Be wise, learn from the experiences
and mistakes of others.
Take courage, go forth, and succeed.
When you feel you can't go on,
take one more step.
You were not sent here to fail.
Always remember these words,
and never forget the feelings
   and thoughts
you have as you read them,
for they are the truth.
They will help you find your own rainbow.

—John William Scott

Always Have a Dream in Your Heart

May you know, in your heart, that
others are always thinking of you.
May you always have rainbows that
follow the rain.
May you celebrate the wonderful things
about you.
And when tomorrow comes, may you
do it all over again.

May you remember how full of smiles
the days can be.
May you believe that what you search for,
you will see.
May you find time to smell the flowers,
and find time to share
the beauty of you.

May you envision today as a gift
and tomorrow as another.
May you add a meaningful page to the
diary of each new day,
and may you make
"living happily ever after . . ."
something that will really come true.

And may you always keep planting
the seeds of your dreams.
Because if you keep
believing in them,
they'll keep trying their best . . .
to blossom for you.

—Collin McCarty

In life, there will always be
many paths to follow;
may you always choose
the right one.
If you give
a part of yourself to life,
the part you receive back
will be so much greater.
Never regret the past,
but learn by it.
Never lose sight of your dreams;
a person who can dream
will always have hope.
Believe in yourself;
if you do, everyone else will.
You have the ability
to accomplish anything,
but never do it at
someone else's expense.
If you can go through life
loving others,
you will have achieved
the greatest success of all.

—Judy LeSage

You Can Make Something Happy Out of Everything That Happens in Life

*L*ife can make choices for us.
Sometimes these choices
seem unhappy or unfair,
   but in the end we control
our own destiny because we can decide
   how people and events affect us.

So much of our happiness lies within
   the choices that we make.
We can accept that life
   isn't the way we want it to be,
   or we can change it so that it will be.
We can walk through the shadows,
   or we can choose to smile
   and seek out the sunlight.
We can create grand dreams
   that never leave the ground,
   or we can be builders
   of dreams that come true.

We can look at only
the negative aspects of ourselves,
or we can lift ourselves up
by being our own best friend.
We can live in the past
or dream about the future,
or we can live for today.
We can give up when the road
becomes difficult,
or we can keep on going
until the view is much better.
The choices in life are endless,
and so is the potential for happiness.

—Nancye Sims

If you know
who you are and
what you want and
why you want it
and if you have
confidence in yourself and
a strong will to obtain your desires and
a very positive attitude
you can make
your life
yours
if you ask

—Susan Polis Schutz

Don't Lose Hope
in Your Dreams

The *days when our dreams*
seem farthest from our reach
are the days
when we need most
*   to have faith in them.*

Even when life is difficult,
we need to remember that
*   we live in a beautiful world*
*   all the same.*
Sometimes we lose sight
*   of how good things can be,*
*   but we must never be blinded by*
*   the discouragement of a single day.*

Things will work out in the end,
   you'll see.
Have patience with yourself
   and with the world.

And keep your dreams
   safe within you.
If you keep believing in them,
   they'll keep trying
      their best to come true.

—Collin McCarty

Believe in Everything
You Can Be

If I could give you
only one thing,
it would be the power
to believe in yourself,
the ability to see your
dreams come true,
and the strength
to make them become real.
I wish you
could see in yourself
what I see in you,
for in you I find
a person with so much potential,
with so many hopes
and dreams,
and an innate ability
to fulfill those dreams.
I believe in you
and in everything
that you can ever be.

—Karen St. Pierre

I wish for you
that the dreams you have realized
remain a constant reminder
of the power within your soul
to exceed the limits
that so few ever do . . .
And that the untold dreams
your heart holds for the future
develop and grow to new heights,
until someday
they, too, are within your grasp.
Most of all, I wish for you
that the dreams you are now
searching for
become dreams no longer,
but that they become real
and very satisfying.

—Jeanne R. Kapsak

Be True to Yourself
in the Pursuit of Your Dreams

In everyone's life
there are moments
of pride and accomplishment
that are remembered forever.

Through the years,
if you set goals and meet each challenge
with enough courage and determination,
you will overcome the many obstacles
that you encounter along the way.

Success is not measured by how well
you fulfill the expectations of others,
but by how honestly you live up to your own.
Be true to yourself
in the pursuit of your dreams,
and you will earn
the right to be proud of your
accomplishments.

—Linda Principe

Always believe in yourself;
do not limit yourself.
Be kind to yourself,
and always believe in
all that is good.
You have all the intelligence
and ability that you need.
You can attain whatever you are after,
even though it may not always
come the way you believe it should.
Be ready to achieve your dreams.
Believe in yourself;
when you are tested
beyond your endurance,
continue and persist.
Hold on to courage.
Let laughter and encouragement
surround you.
The world has much to give;
always think big,
and keep your head and heart open,
for then you will receive
all of life's gifts.

—Dorothy Hewitt

We Need to Feel More

We need to feel more to understand others
We need to love more to be loved back
We need to cry more to cleanse ourselves
We need to laugh more to enjoy ourselves

We need to establish the values of
honesty and fairness
when interacting with people
We need to establish a strong ethical basis
as a way of life

We need to see more
than our own little fantasies
We need to hear more
and listen to the needs of others
We need to give more and take less
We need to share more and own less

We need to realize the importance of the family
as a backbone to stability
We need to look more
and realize that we are not so different
from one another

We need to create a world where
we can all peacefully live
the life we choose
We need to create a world where
we can once again trust each other

—Susan Polis Schutz

Your Dreams Are
Within Your Reach

*The steps that
have brought you this far
have shown you that
you have the ability to accomplish
   your goals
and the strength to hold on
when all seems lost or hopeless.
You have the wisdom to know
that the determination to go on
only comes from within.
It is a mixture of faith in God
and complete trust in yourself
that will turn dreams into reality.
Most important is your heart.
Without that,
a dream can never make it past
just being a wish.*

—Susan M. Pavlis

Always Hold on to Your Dreams

*Don't let go of hope in your dreams.
Hope gives you the strength
to keep going
when you feel like giving up.
Don't ever quit believing in yourself.
As long as you believe you can,
you will have a reason for trying.
Don't let anyone hold your happiness
in their hands; hold it in yours,
so it will always be within your reach.
Don't measure success or failure
by material wealth,
but by how you feel;
our feelings determine
the richness of our lives.
Don't let bad moments overcome you;
be patient, and they will pass.
Don't hesitate to reach out for help;
we all need it from time to time.*

Don't run away from love but towards love,
because it is our deepest joy.
Don't wait for what you want
to come to you.
Go after it with all that you are,
knowing that life will meet you halfway.
Don't feel like you've lost
when plans and dreams fall short of your hopes.
Anytime you learn something new
about yourself or about life,
you have progressed.
Don't do anything that takes away
from your self-respect.
Feeling good about yourself
is essential to feeling good about life.
Don't ever forget how to laugh
or be too proud to cry.
It is by doing both
that we live life to its fullest.

—Nancye Sims

Now is the time for you to celebrate the accomplishments of the dreams you have worked so hard to realize.

And now is the time to begin to pursue the next path, to reach out for the next star, and to achieve the things that are so important to you.

Always keep your dreams alive.

And keep them coming true.

—Collin McCarty

You are an exceptional person,
and I wish so many things for you.
May you continue to dream
and believe in the magic of life.
May your dreams be inspired,
and may you pursue them
with enthusiasm.
May you know that success
isn't measured in material things,
but in joy.
May you be gentle with yourself
whenever you fail,
and may every corner of your life
be filled with love
and happiness,
today and in the years to come.

—Marian Tomberlin

Always Believe in Your
Unlimited Potential

*B*elieve in yourself.
You have the ability to attain
whatever you seek; within you
is every potential you can imagine.
Always aim higher than
you believe you can reach.
So often, you'll discover
that when your talents are set free
by your imagination,
you can achieve any goal.
If people offer you their help or wisdom
as you go through life,
accept it gratefully.
You can learn much from those
who have gone before you.
But never be afraid or hesitant
to step off the accepted path
and strike off on your own,
if your heart tells you it's right.
Always believe you will ultimately
succeed at whatever you do.
Regard failure as a perfect opportunity
to show yourself how strong you truly are.
Believe in persistence, discipline,
   and always believe in yourself.
You are meant to be
      whatever you dream of becoming.

—Edmund O'Neill

Within You Is the Strength
to Make Your Dreams Come True

You are stronger than you think—
remember to stand tall.
Every challenge in your life
    helps you to grow.
Every problem you encounter
    strengthens your mind and your soul.
Every trouble you overcome
    increases your understanding of life.
When all your troubles weigh heavily
    on your shoulders,
remember that beneath the burden
    you can stand tall,
because you are never given
    more than you can handle—
and you are stronger
    than you think.

—Lisa Wroble

You Have So Many Dreams to Look Forward To

Our lives have so many
backward glances in them,
don't they . . .
Thinking back to how things
were and how things might
have been . . .

There's nothing wrong with
thinking back; but it probably is
a mistake to dwell on
    the past "what ifs."
Instead, we should concentrate
on today, on tomorrow,
and on the tomorrows yet to be.

There are a lot of beautiful days
  yet to come.

The past is past . . .
  but tomorrow will last forever.
Never stop hoping that
  each tomorrow
will fill your heart with love
  and laughter,
your days with dreams come true,
  and your life with so much
    happiness to look forward to.

—*Adrian Rogers*

For every dream in your heart,
  I wish you greater inspiration.

For every hope you seek,
I wish you unexpected miracles.

For every opportunity awaiting you,
I wish you an extra chance.

For every challenge you meet,
I wish you a piece of your destiny.

Your greatest aspiration is but the
beginning of all that you have to offer.

So reach beyond yourself . . .
and let your heart carry you ever higher.

—Barbara Vecqueray

Go After What You Want in Life

*N*ever give up on
who you think you can be.
There is a lifetime of potential
within you
just waiting to be discovered.

Life takes us down many roads;
it's up to you to take control
of where you want to go.
Where you are now is where
you have taken yourself;
you are never in a situation
you aren't supposed to be in.

Go after what you want in life,
and do it with the knowledge
that you are capable of looking
beyond any horizon you choose.
Every day is your own;
be true to who you are.

—Whitney Miles

Within You Is
the Promise of the Future

Within you is an ideal,
a voice of strength,
and a promise of achievement
still to come.
Within your hands
are special gifts and talents.
Within your mind is
the source of your dreams.
Within you is the strength to carry
your dreams to completion.
Within your heart is the desire
to meet the world on your own terms.
You are strong; you are wise;
you have a dream.
You have spirit and confidence;
you have faith.
You are your own person,
and you always will be.
Within you
is something so precious and rare.
Within you is the promise of the future.

—Jean Lamey

You Can Make Your Dreams Come True

*L*ook within.
And listen to your heart.
You can do it.
You can reach that goal.
You can make that new reality
    instead of accepting things
        the way they used to be.

You can do it.

All of your highest hopes are with you.
Nothing will hold you back
    but your own fears.
And if those fears were created by you,
    they can be dealt with by you . . .
        and said good-bye to.

You can do it.
Say it to yourself, and believe it in your heart.
Make every single day a positive start
    leading to a better and bright tomorrow.

You can do it.

You really can.

—Alin Austin

Reach Out for
Everything You Want to Achieve

*T*ake the time to explore
the world around you.
You helped to create it,
and you are capable of changing it.
Nothing can keep you
from becoming whatever you're
capable of dreaming.
Everything surrounding you
is just another chance
to discover something new,
so don't hesitate to reach out
and become all that you're capable
of becoming.
Every new phase you encounter
is a continuation of what
you've already begun.
The only limitations are those
you allow yourself to believe in.
So go ahead . . .
    and reach for everything
    you want to achieve.

—Lee Wheeler

You can be anything
you want to be.
Don't ever let anyone
discourage you in your dreams,
no matter what.
You have your dream within you;
no one can take it away.
Believing in yourself
will take you as far
in life
as you want to go,
especially if that belief
is as strong as
the confidence I have in you.

—Ann Rudacille

Believe in Yourself

Believe in yourself;
believe in your mind
and all the dreams, intelligence,
and determination within you.
You can accomplish anything.
You have so much open to you,
so please don't give up on what you want
*   from life*
or from yourself.
Please don't put away the dreams inside
*   of you.*
You have the power to make them real.
You have the power to make yourself
*   exactly what you want to be.*
Believe in yourself,
*   and nothing will be beyond your reach.*

—Joleen K. Fox

Success Is Achieved
One Step at a Time

*It is not the final success
that remains in your heart
or brings you satisfaction;
it is the day-after-day dedication
and endless belief
you have in yourself
that endures and continues
to push you on.
It is looking ahead, not behind;
it is knowing that
by taking one step forward,
other steps will follow,
and the journey you are on
will lead you to
wherever you want to go.*

—Deanna Beisser

Each Day Can Be
the Beginning of a
Wonderful Future for You

*B*ehind you lies a long road travelled,
and each turn in that road
led up to this day:
    the memory of your experiences,
    the effort you have exerted,
    the benefits you have gained,
    and the new friendships
        you have made along the way.

Before you lie brand-new horizons
and adventures:
    new roads to travel
    and dreams to fulfill,
    plans to satisfy,
    hopes to carry out,
    and fresh goals to explore.

As you take the new paths before you,
may all the dreams, hopes, and plans
that you carry in your heart today
be the beginning of a new pathway
that leads to the goals you deserve
in the future.

        —Judith J. Yerman

May Tomorrow Bring You
Every Dream in Your Heart

*F*ollow your heart;
never surrender your dreams.
Constantly work towards your goals.
Believe in yourself and always be truthful.
Take time to enjoy life's pleasures.
Keep your mind open to new experiences.
Think before acting,
but don't forget the joys of spontaneity.
Make your own decisions.
Look out for yourself,
but remember that you
share this universe with others.
Look for the good in others—everybody
has their own song to sing.
Live each moment to the fullest,
for a moment too soon becomes a memory.
Look for opportunities, not guarantees.
Hope for the best.
Give people a chance to love you,
for that is how you learn to love.
Live your life for yourself,
but always be considerate of others.
Believe in tomorrow, for it holds the key
to your dreams.

—Melissa Ososki

*N*o matter what you do,
don't ever stop believing
in better times
and brighter days.

There are too many possibilities,
too many opportunities,
and too many dreams
to ever lose hope.
When times are bad,
they can only get better.
When things are okay,
a little encouragement will
help them stay that way.

And the horizon of tomorrow
may hold surprises that will
make things better than you
ever imagined.

So don't give up hope,
and don't ever stop believing in
the things that you can do.

It could be that
one of your dreams
is just waiting for you
to make it come true.

—Collin McCarty

You Have the Power
to Make Your Dreams Come True

This life is yours
Believe in yourself
Take the power
to choose what you want to do
and do it well
Take the power
to love what you want in life
and love it honestly
Take the power
to walk in the forest
and be a part of nature
Take the power
to control your own life
No one else can do it for you
Nothing is too good for you
You deserve the best
Take the power
to make your life
healthy
exciting
worthwhile
and very happy
Take the power
to create your own dreams
and make them come true

—Susan Polis Schutz

Promise Yourself Only the Best

*P*romise yourself
to dream more and hesitate less.
To believe in yourself more
and judge yourself less by
the accomplishments of others.
To appreciate your family
and friends
for all the wonderful ways
they make your life better.
To accept life as it comes
and truly make each day special.
To become more independent
and more willing to change.
To fill every day
with special times
and make your dreams come true.

—Deanna Beisser

Have a Happy . . . Everything!

May you always know
how appreciated you are.
May you never forget what a blessing
you've become to a world that could
use more people like you.
May you reap the rewards of kindness.
May your sunshine always shine through.

May love walk by your side.
May friendship sing in your smile.
May opportunity remember to knock on your
door and surprise you once in a while.
May your memories be ones that you
wouldn't trade.
May your hopes and dreams
find ways of coming true.

May you have
a "Happy . . . Everything!"

—Collin McCarty

ACKNOWLEDGMENTS

The following is a partial list of authors whom the publisher especially wishes to thank for permission to reprint their works.

Randey Fisher for "Always Be True to Yourself."

John William Scott for "You Have Within You the Courage to Achieve Your Goals."

Nancye Sims for "You Can Make Something Happy Out of Everything That Happens in Life."

Jeanne R. Kapsak for "I wish for you . . ."

Linda Principe for "Be True to Yourself in the Pursuit of Your Dreams."

Dorothy Hewitt for "Always believe in yourself . . ."

Marian Tomberlin for "You are an exceptional person . . ."

Ann Rudacille for "You can be anything . . ."

Deanna Beisser for "Success Is Achieved One Step at a Time."

Judith J. Yerman for "Each Day Can Be the Beginning of a Wonderful Future for You."